Also by Toby Knobel Fluek

Passover As I Remember It

Memories *of* My Life *in a* Polish Village
1930–1949

Paintings, drawings, and text by

Toby Knobel Fluek

Foreword by Rakhmiel Peltz, PhD, PhD

THE EXPERIMENT

NEW YORK

MEMORIES OF MY LIFE IN A POLISH VILLAGE, 1930–1949
Text and illustrations copyright © 1990 by Toby Knobel Fluek
Foreword copyright © 2024 by Rakhmiel Peltz, PhD, PhD

Originally published by Alfred A. Knopf in 1990. This edition first published by
The Experiment, LLC, in 2024.

The Experiment, LLC
220 East 23rd Street, Suite 600
New York, NY 10010-4658
theexperimentpublishing.com

THE EXPERIMENT and its colophon are registered trademarks of The Experiment,
LLC. Many of the designations used by manufacturers and sellers to distinguish their
products are claimed as trademarks. Where those designations appear in this book and
The Experiment was aware of a trademark claim, the designations have been capitalized.

The Experiment's books are available at special discounts when purchased in bulk for
premiums and sales promotions as well as for fundraising or educational use. For details,
contact us at info@theexperimentpublishing.com.

Library of Congress Cataloging-in-Publication Data available upon request

ISBN 978-1-891011-68-9
Ebook ISBN 978-1-891011-69-6

Cover and text design by Beth Bugler
Author photograph by Lillian Fluek Finkler and Steven Finkler

Manufactured in China

First printing May 2024
10 9 8 7 6 5 4 3 2 1

In loving memory of my family and my husband's family
who perished during the Holocaust,
and
to my dear grandchildren, David and Gary,
knowing you will always remember

Contents

Foreword to the New Edition
by Rakhmiel Peltz, PhD, PhD

From my first viewing of the film *Image Before My Eyes*, a documentary history of Jews in modern Poland until World War II that relies heavily on photographs and testimonies of Holocaust survivors, I was captivated by the initial vignette, which focuses on life in an agricultural village as depicted in the words and paintings of Toby Knobel Fluek. In 1990 and 1994, two art books appeared in a bookstore on the main downtown shopping street of the city of Northampton in western Massachusetts, where I was living with my wife and two young children. I purchased these books, *Memories of My Life in a Polish Village, 1930–1949* and *Passover As I Remember It*, with the intention of reading them to our children when they grew older, since they were grandchildren of two Holocaust survivors, my wife's parents, and I felt that Toby Knobel Fluek's warm, colorful oil and pastel paintings of rich, traditional Jewish life were the best vehicles for introducing children to the world that was destroyed and to the Holocaust.

In 1995, I met Toby Fluek at a conference of Holocaust survivors in Miami Beach, where she and her husband spent part of the winter at that time. I was then a professor at Columbia University, heading the Yiddish Studies Program, which included an intensive summer course of study. I invited Toby to give a talk, but she told me she was busy painting in the summer, and since she did not drive, getting there from the Catskills survivor bungalow colony was a challenge. I later moved to Drexel University to establish its Judaic Studies Program and invited Toby to speak to a class on the history of the Holocaust. I had sensed all along that Toby had a unique message and that her images and presentation would be unforgettable for students as an introduction to the study of the Holocaust and to Jewish life and culture. I asked a student of mine who was a film and video major to record the course meeting. Over lunch that day in November 2001, we discussed the need for a film about Toby's life and art because I was fearful that her books would go out of print. I argued that a documentary would enable instructors to invoke a Toby presentation whenever needed, and everyone around the table agreed. I could not foresee that this multimedia effort would involve me as producer and project director for the next six and a half years.

My ten-year friendship with Toby Knobel Fluek enriched my life forever. Besides the many filming sessions, Toby and I talked every week on the telephone in Yiddish. I called her Toby, but she always addressed me as Dr. Peltz. She was perpetually in a good mood, yet earnest. She understood that she had a message to share. Since her childhood years, she loved to paint and draw, but from the time her mother suggested to Toby in about 1960 that she should "paint the farm," she couldn't stop. People would ask her to paint something for them, but her response was always, "I can't, I'm busy, I have to paint the farm." It was not by chance that Toby's mother had this influence on her. Very few young Jews survived the war with a parent. For a year, Toby had been in hiding all alone in the woods and barns near her village of Czernica after escaping from the Brody ghetto. Her mother hid separately because they realized that it would be better if they begged for food on their own. Yet, after the war, Toby's mother was an influential force in the family for Toby; her husband, Max; and their daughter, Lilli. This unique family clung to Toby, her cooking, her stories, her songs, her cheerfulness, her art, and her lessons, and they shared these with their younger relatives, including Toby's son-in-law, Steven, and her grandsons, Gary and David.

But her lessons are not only alive within her family: They have seeded new understandings of the Holocaust and Jewish life and culture among students in classrooms, museum visitors, and readers of her books. I had the privilege of interviewing Toby many times. Along with her images in this book, her spoken words live with me: the star of David atop the farmhouse roof (page 3) and "We were proud to be Jews"; the kitchen as the center of family life (page 5) and "I did my homework at that table"; her father reading with her (page 32) and "After *Shabbos* lunch, my father would teach me to read Hebrew"; the vibrant colors of the mortar and pestle and ingredients of the Passover *charoses* (page 41) and "This was my father's job"; her time in hiding, when it was raining cats and dogs (page 102) and "I was going to give up, but I changed and decided I was going to live." Toby's lessons led me to interview other survivors to explore the role of their memories of a beloved and meaningful Jewish life at home before the war in fortifying their will to live. The Nazis were not able to extinguish the humanity and shared culture within these Jews.

Toby's influence also inspired me to investigate the difficulty that future generations of groups that are victims of genocide have in teaching about the life that was destroyed. I had not understood this difficulty, even though for decades I had been studying, researching, and teaching Yiddish and the history of the world that was destroyed during the Holocaust. Future generations internalize the feeling of being worthy of being herded into a ghetto and thrown into an oven. These groups need help in appreciating and teaching the history of their victimized cultures, whether this relates to pre-genocide Rwanda, the former Yugoslavia, or Native American life. Growing from my learning from Toby, I generated an educational program, Alive! Educational Restitution After Genocide (alivetobyssunshine.com). In 2001, we were certain that Toby's books were destined to be out of print. But now, in 2024, we welcome the appearance of *Memories* in its new edition.

Rakhmiel Peltz, PhD, PhD, is Professor Emeritus of Sociolinguistics in the Department of Communication at Drexel University and Founding Director of the Judaic Studies Program, which he led for twenty years. He is a developmental biologist who specialized in molecular and cellular biology and a Yiddish linguist who focuses on the social history of Yiddish language and culture. Currently, he is writing a book comparing standardizers in biomedical research and Yiddish language standardizers who fought for a secure future for the Jewish people in modern history.

Memories *of* My Life *in a* Polish Village
1930–1949

My Family at Work

Our Farm

I was born and grew up on this farm in a rural village named Czernica in eastern Poland. My father's family had been there for generations.

There were ten Jewish families in the village. The total population was about 250 families, Polish and Ukrainian. There was no synagogue or *cheder* (Hebrew school) in the village, and services were held in our house on the Sabbath and holidays. When we needed a *shochet* (ritual slaughterer) or rabbi, we had to go to Podkamien, the nearby *shtetl* (town).

The Foyer

The foyer was the main entrance to our house, leading to the kitchen and the two large rooms on either side. It also served as our washroom. The large brass basin was the sink. One towel was used by six. I had two older sisters, Surcie and Lajcie, an older brother, Aron, and there were my parents.

The stepladder went up to the attic. In the attic was our treasure chest, a large wooden box with clothes from American relatives. At the age of thirteen, I remember wearing a navy blue coat from America. I was so happy nobody was my equal. It became new after my sister resewed it inside out because the color had faded on the outside.

Our Kitchen

In this room my mother cooked the meals and baked the bread, and the wash-woman did the laundry here. Mother baked bread for a whole week at a time. The kneading of the dough took a lot of elbow grease; it was done in a large wooden tub.

There were two wood-burning stoves for cooking and an oven for baking. Every farmhouse had similar stoves. The poor lived in only one large room like this one, with a bed in the corner.

My Father

Father was a born farmer, and knew little else, although he did a little *hundling*, which means peddling. Mother was the businesswoman in the family. Father worked all day in the fields with the hired help. He tied the bundles of cut wheat and placed them in special stacks to be dried in the sun. Later he threshed the wheat with primitive tools similar to those used in biblical times. My mother and sister helped Father shred straw to feed the animals.

Aron

***

My brother, Aron, boarded in Podkamien, attending cheder and elementary school. He used to come for the holidays and special occasions. At his Bar Mitzvah, cake and schnapps were served at Sabbath services in our house. In the villages, that was the extent of a Bar Mitzvah celebration. After his Bar Mitzvah, Aron said his prayers daily, wearing his *tefillin* (phylacteries).

Surcie Fitting a Dress

My sister Surcie was known as the best dressmaker in Czernica. She made the clothes for the intelligentsia and the wealthier people. She worked hard to make a well-fitting garment. Surcie made some blouses for the peasants too, and they in return worked for us in the fields. (The long, gathered skirts the women made for themselves by hand.) Note the ark on the left of the drawing. The Sabbath and holiday services were held in the same room.

Lajcie Ironing

My sister Lajcie did most of the household chores. She ironed, cleaned, mended, and helped Mother with the cooking.

On Thursdays she always had scraped knuckles from the metal potato grater. Mother used to bake big pans of potato pudding for the Sabbath.

Lajcie needed a lot of dental work. To earn the money, she took care of an elderly person in Brody. But it was considered a *shande* (shame) to be a maid. My parents were embarrassed and kept it a secret.

Rekindling the Embers

The iron was kept hot by filling it with hot wood embers. In order for the iron to maintain the heat, you had constantly to wave it high in the air to agitate the embers. Then every half hour or so we had to refill it with more hot embers from the wood-burning stove.

It was a painstaking job to iron in those days.

Apprentice

Surcie had two girls working as apprentices: Ruchcie from the nearby village of Pankowic and Jewka from our village. They came for one year to our house, five days a week, to learn the trade of dressmaking.

Some dressmakers had their apprentices do household work such as cleaning or carrying wood and water. Surcie never took advantage of her apprentices.

Surcie and Lonie

My sister Surcie was in love with Lonie Halpern, a neighbor of ours. They kept company for five years, but they couldn't get married because Lonie had an older single sister. In those days parents didn't permit a younger sibling to get married first, especially a boy.

Lonie's sister Julia had a fiancé in Hamburg, Germany. He was supposed to come to Czernica to marry her. Through some mishap with his visa he was not able to come.

I remember my father arguing with Surcie that she was wasting her time with Lonie, that he wouldn't get married until his older sister did. Mother understood Surcie better—she knew they were very much in love. Unfortunately, the war started, and they never got married.

Going to School

At the age of six, I started elementary school in the first grade. The school day began with a religious prayer, and the other children crossed themselves. I felt uncomfortable, and some of my classmates teased me, saying that I would have to cross myself too. That upset me very much; I was the only Jewish student in the school.

The second problem was that we had six days of school. My family and I were Orthodox Jews, but this did not excuse me from going to school on the Sabbath. I attended the classes on those days but didn't write. I enjoyed school and received awards for excellent schoolwork. A teacher discovered my art ability and advised my parents to send me to an art school. Unfortunately, this was just not possible.

Red Potatoes

Potatoes were the main source of nourishment. We grew them in our field. They were used in countless main dishes. We ate boiled, baked, and mashed potatoes, potato pudding, potato pirogen. Potato soup with browned flour was excellent for a good heartburn! There was a song we used to sing: "Sunday Potatoes, Monday Potatoes, Tuesday and Wednesday Potatoes, Thursday Potatoes, Friday Potatoes, *Shabbos in cholent* (Sabbath stew) also Potatoes!"

©1928 TOBY FLUEK

Making Potato Latkes

O ur family enjoyed a potato *latke* (pancake) dinner, but Mother complained bitterly about making one. The latkes always disappeared before she could bring them to the table. When my brother and I were very young, we would grab the pancakes from the large clay bowl. Because oil was expensive, Mother made the pancakes on the iron sheet on top of the stove. To make them tastier, a few drops of oil and crushed garlic were added after they were cooked. Pancakes fried in oil were eaten only on Passover and Chanukah.

My Uncle Mordche

My uncle Mordche made a living buying eggs from the peasants and selling them to the city merchants. All day he walked along the dirt roads, at times ankle-deep in the mud, to buy a few eggs from a peasant. Peddling was a way of life. He always had a sad look on his face. He had two daughters of marriageable age, and to be poor and without a dowry was a good reason to be sad.

Eventually he married off his daughters through a matchmaker. The older daughter, Sheiwa, married a widower with three children. Chana, the younger one, married a boy from Podchajew, a town near the Russian border. That was no great honor either: the people from that region were called *Fonie gonif*, the Russian thieves.

Aunt Rifka

Aunt Rifka was a simple woman, a homebody, very much like my father. She kept very much to the old ways of dress, while my mother was more up-to-date.

She didn't know how to hundle and couldn't help her husband in the business. Aunt Rifka and Uncle Mordche were one of the very few families in the village that didn't own their own house. My parents helped them out with food, and the relatives from America sent clothes.

Preparations for the Sabbath

Grocery Shopping

Most of the essential food was grown on the farm; we had to buy only a few products. These were oil, sugar, salt, pepper, cinnamon, and kerosene for the lamp. Candy was a luxury. To buy oil, you had to bring your own bottle to the grocery for them to fill it up. There were no paper bags, so the grocery used brown paper or sometimes newspaper to make paper cones, and the sugar, salt, or whatever, was poured from big sacks into the cones for us to carry home. Since newspaper was scarce in the village, a piece of cloth tied to a bundle was often used for grocery shopping.

Koshering the Meat

The salted meat was placed on an oval holder woven from birch-tree twigs, which rested on the large brass basin. Mother lit two candles, whether it was day or night, so that she might have better light to be sure the salt was spread evenly on all sides, a tradition carried over from her mother. Chicken and *flanken* (beef) we ate only for Sabbath meals. A midweek meat meal, we had once in a while when Father slaughtered an animal. He sold most of the meat, and then we would have a treat, dinner made from the lungs, heart, pancreas, liver, and cheeks.

Drelis, a chilled stew from calves' feet, was a Sabbath delicacy, and the small intestines would make another meal.

Baking Challah

Every Jewish family would save a whole week's earnings to prepare a good meal and baked goods for the Sabbath. We never had cake on weekdays. I enjoyed watching Mother braid the *challah* (a special white bread), and I learned how to bake.

Mother also baked for the other villages to get a little extra income. For Easter, the peasants used to order large braided white breads called *Paska*. For the intellectuals—the priest, the engineer—Mother baked round sponge cakes.

The Galician Chassid

On Saturdays and holidays my father used to wear a *shtreimel*, a fur hat, to attend religious services. This was mostly a custom of the Chassidim (an Orthodox sect) and the ultra-Orthodox Jews of Galicia (the area of Poland my village was in).

The hats were made from mink tails. The rich Jews had them made from expensive, especially raised minks, and the poor wore skimpy shtreimels fashioned from wild mink tails.

Lighting Sabbath Candles

F riday afternoons the wood-burning oven was heated, and the cholent was placed there to cook overnight for the Sabbath meal. The house was cleaned, and everyone dressed in their good Sabbath clothes and freshly polished shoes. Before sundown Mother blessed the Sabbath candles. The brass candlesticks, she had received as a dowry from her parents. We had no services Friday nights. Father said the evening prayer alone, and the festive Friday night meal was served.

Teaching

Saturdays after the big noon meal, Father used to teach me to read Hebrew. There was no library in the village, therefore books weren't easily available. If I read a Polish book on Saturday, which my friend lent me from her own library, Father would say, "On the Sabbath you don't read Polish books, on the Sabbath you read Hebrew." He was only interested that I should know enough Hebrew to read the prayer book on the High Holidays.

The Tallis

The *tallis*, or prayer shawl, was worn daily at morning prayers, on the Sabbath, and on holidays. In Europe, when a boy reached the age of three, his father wrapped a tallis around him and carried him to the cheder for the first time. A man was given his own prayer shawl when he got married.

My father had a large woolen tallis with a wide silverhead strip. When the *tzitzis* (fringes) had worn out from daily use, Father replaced them with new woolen tzitzis he knotted himself.

The Holidays

Cleaning Utensils

Housecleaning for Passover started weeks before the holiday: airing out the clothes from the winter dampness, washing out all the baking utensils, whitewashing the stoves, and covering the earthen floors with a new coat of yellow mud that we dug up from the backyard and mixed with water.

The old worn benches were scrubbed with a brush, using sand as a cleanser. I used to sweep the earthen floors with the broom my father made from birch twigs. I was young and could hardly hold it in my small hands—the broom was as tall as me.

Painting the Floor

The earthen floors needed extra care in the spring. My father scraped off the accumulated dirt near the entrance door with a shovel. Then Lajcie painted the floor with the yellow mud.

I felt bad that Lajcie did most of the heavy housework, but I was the youngest and spoiled and did not volunteer much help. My job was to keep the clothing closets neat, scrubbing and polishing everybody's shoes before the Sabbath and holidays.

Passover Pots

According to Orthodox Jewish law, a separate set of dishes, pots, and silverware was required for Passover.

Before the holidays we unpacked the box of Passover dishes from the attic. Each piece had a history. Grandma Chaje-Dine gave the bowl with the red flower design, and the white enamel pot came from Aunt Matel.

In those days, pots were received as wedding gifts. Dishes were also handed down from mother to daughter. The enamel pots that we used all year eventually developed holes, but nothing was discarded. Father patched them up with lead, and we used them again for cooking.

In an emergency, a small hole would be sealed by pulling a tiny piece of cloth through it, and the pot would be used for storage. This was done because a housewife didn't own extra pots.

The Basket with Eggs

W̲e started preparing for Passover weeks in advance. Mother saved eggs, and the geese were fattened and slaughtered. Goose fat was prepared to be used with mashed potatoes, in soups, or spread on matzoh. The *grieven*, little pieces of browned fat that couldn't be preserved, were enjoyed right away on a piece of bread. Dozens of eggs were used for Passover meals. We even gobbled up plain hard-boiled eggs. We waited all year to eat matzoh balls and noodles made from eggs.

Making Charoses

The brass mortar and pestle had been handed down from generation to generation. During the year they were used to crush cinnamon, pepper, and garlic. Each year, for Passover, they were *kashered* (made kosher) according to Orthodox law, to crush the nuts for *charoses*. Chopped apples, nuts, and wine made up the mixture for charoses for the *seder* (Passover meal).

Making charoses was my father's job, and we weren't allowed to taste it before the seder.

This delicious treat is a reminder of the mortar used by the enslaved Jews to build pyramids for the Pharaohs in Egypt.

Our Seder

My father conducted the seder lying on the bed, leaning on the pillows. He was dressed in the *kapote*, a black silk coat with a silk string at his waist. Alongside the bed we placed a long table covered with a white damask tablecloth. Everything on the table was *yomtovdik* (festive). My mother, my sisters, and I dressed in our best clothes and sat on a long bench, with my brother next to my father. The youngest son of the family, in our case my brother, asked the Four Questions.

When I was little I remember waiting impatiently to drink the wine and to eat the delicious meal. My father chanted the Haggadah in Hebrew in the same manner and melody as his father had done. I, being the youngest, opened the door for Elijah. I remember watching the Elijah cup to see if any wine was missing. Mother told Elijah-stories of her youth.

Kreplach

On *Shavuos* (a harvest holiday), we decorated our house with twigs and greenery, placing small branches around the picture frames on the walls and a bouquet of wildflowers on the table.

On this holiday, which also celebrated the receiving of the Ten Commandments, it was customary to eat only dairy foods, as a reminder that when Moses came down from the mountain, the children of Israel wanted to celebrate but had to do it without meat since there was no time to make it kosher.

Before Shavuos, Mother would make extra farmer cheese and sour cream and store it in the cellar, which kept it cool (our way of refrigeration). Our favorite dish for the Shavuos midday meal was cheese-filled *kreplach* (dumplings).

The Candlesticks

Before Rosh Hashanah and Yom Kippur (New Year's and the Day of Atonement), while blessing the *yom-tov* (holiday) candles, Mother recited the prayers with loud sobs. It was a very emotional moment. As a little girl I was anxious to know why she cried. Mother explained, "God listens to the prayers if they are recited with deep emotion."

The Baal T'fila

For Rosh Hashanah and Yom Kippur we had a *Baal T'fila* (leader in prayer) come from Podkamien to conduct the services in our house. It was a very somber holiday. Before *Kol Nidre* (a special prayer for Yom Kippur), my father used to bring a few bundles of straw and spread it on the earthen floors of the large room for the men and in the kitchen for the women. Since people weren't allowed to wear leather shoes on Yom Kippur, the straw kept our stocking feet warm. At night it was shoved in a corner and covered with a sheet to be used as a mattress. My uncle Mordche stayed with us because it was customary to sleep over in the place of worship to watch the *Yahrzeit* candles, the homemade candles that were lit to remember the dead.

Shlogn Kapores

A ceremony for repentance. This was done the morning before Kol Nidre. What made this prayer so different was that a chicken was used as a scapegoat symbol. As my sisters and I said the prayer for forgiveness for our sins, Surcie would swing the chicken over our heads. Later my parents gave charity to the poor. Father brought the *shochet* (kosher slaughterer) from the next shtetl by horse and buggy. All the Jewish housewives brought their *kapores* ("sacrificial fowl") to our farm to slaughter the same morning for the feast before Yom Kippur.

Succoth

S*uccoth* is the fall festival when Jews recall their forty years in the desert by eating in an open shelter (*succah*) like the ones used in their wanderings.

Our succah was different from anybody else's because it was made in the foyer. Father removed the shingles from the roof right above the opening to the attic, which was in the foyer. He placed the tallest cornstalks to cover the opening. There were no special decorations in the succah, only a table and two chairs. Father took pride in the fact that Mother did not have to carry food outside as other women did. When I was young I wanted to eat in the succah, but Mother told me that only men ate in there. That is how it was in our village.

Chanukah

In our home, there was a brass Chanukah lamp, a *menorah*. Father placed a cotton string in each compartment with oil and then lit it. My parents gave me Chanukah *gelt* (money). Some poor people didn't own a menorah, and so they had to make one. They took a small potato and cut off the top and bottom, which made it stand. They chiseled out a hole and placed a candle in it. People learned to manage with what was available.

Purim

What I remember most about Purim is reading the *Megillah*, "Queen Esther's scroll," by the dingy light of a kerosene lamp, and the preparation for baking *hamantaschen* (a Purim pastry). Crushing the poppy seeds for the filling was fun. The poppy seeds were emptied from the pods that grew in our garden into a big clay bowl. While Lajcie held the bowl, Mother added sugar and crushed the mixture in a circular motion with a large wooden utensil shaped like a head, called a *makuheen*.

I remember if I tried to *nosh* (taste) the mixture from the makuheen, Mother used to say, "If you nosh from the makuheen you will marry a bald-headed husband!" I also remember the saying, "Today is Purim, tomorrow it's gone, give me a penny and throw me out."

Our Neighbors

Shimon Katz

Although we were a small village, the class system was strong. Czernica had ten Jewish families and four classes of people. There was the *oisher* (rich man), the *Talmud-Chuchem* (educated in the Bible), the *balbatisher* (the respectable middle class), and the *kapzen*, or poor man.

Shimon, a neighbor of ours, was a poor man who made his living hundling. He would go to different villages to buy flax, horsehair, and feathers, and then sell them. When Chaim Parnes from Ponikwa came to buy cows for slaughtering, Shimon took him to the peasants who had animals to sell. His son Abram also peddled. Abram fell in love with my cousin Dusia Knobel. But her mother, Tema, was furious because she didn't want her daughter to marry a poor boy. She put up a big struggle to discourage the love affair. After a long battle, Abram succeeded, and they got married in 1939. A year later their son Srulek was born.

Hersh Milrom

Hersh Milrom was the oisher, the rich man. He had a grocery store that his daughter tended. In one large room he sold groceries, leather for shoes and boots, and cigarettes. Everyone had shoes and boots made to order, so the leather business was very profitable. Although it was difficult to get a concession to sell cigarettes, Hersh Milrom managed to get one. He also owned farmland and hired peasants to work in the fields and in the barn.

Katerina

Our neighbor Katerina and her children helped us with many chores. Katerina used to sift the wheat in the barn. Her son often shredded it. And her daughter, Jewka, used to run errands for us on the Sabbath, when we could not do any work. Wintertimes she made the fire in the oven to heat the room. In return, Mother gave Katerina some money and stitched over her handsewn linen shirts. Very few people had sewing machines.

Cutting the Oats

Wasyl, our neighbor, worked in the fields for us, cutting the oats and hay with a scythe. Since some fields were about two kilometers away, Wasyl used his horse and buggy to get the wheat and hay to our barn. In the early 1930s my parents owned a horse and two cows. As the economy got worse, Father sold the horse and one cow. The remaining cow supplied our family with milk.

Karolczycha

Karolczycha was the self-taught doctor in the village. She grew all kinds of herbs in her garden. She dried them and, when called upon, treated sick people. She owned a book on herbal medicine and read up on herbal cures. Not too many women her age knew how to read at all. Karolczycha was childless and loved to help people. At times she would take a sick girl into her house for a few days and treat her with homemade remedies so that the girl's family could go about their work.

Woman Carrying Water

There were natural springs along the river flowing through the center of the village. The women carried pails of fresh spring water from the cement wells to their homes for drinking and washing. The older peasants wore long skirts and scarves tied under their chins while the younger generation wore dresses mid-calf length. Most women used to go barefoot.

Washing

A few times a year and before the holiday, Katerina washed our linen sheets, heavy bedding, and linen towels in a big wooden washtub. The water was warmed on the wood-burning stove in a large metal pot. She used a wooden washboard to scrub the laundry, and then it was boiled with washing soda to get it clean. She rinsed it in the river, beating it with a wooden board. In wintertime her apron froze.

It took two days to do the laundry.

Spinning

The peasant women spun the flax into thread, and the weaver made the thread into linen on a homemade wooden loom. To whiten the linen the women carried it to the river, wet it, and spread it out on the grass to bleach it in the sun. It took days to get needed results. Sheets, towels, tablecloths, aprons, and working shirts were made out of linen.

We hand-embroidered the towels with red and black cross-stitching and sometimes added fringes.

Plucking Feathers

During the winter evenings, Mother would invite our neighbors, the peasant women, to a feather-plucking party. They sat around the table telling jokes and stories, having a good time while the work was done. Afterward Mother served baked potatoes with herring.

The feathers were used to make feather beds and pillows. Pastry brushes were fashioned from geese and duck tails, and we made feather dusters from the wings.

Wasyl Taking a Sunday Stroll

Wasyl used to visit my father, and another neighbor would join them. They sat and reminisced about World War I or talked politics. One of their main topics then was how America could help Poland with the economy. I was always full of curiosity and liked to listen to their stories.

Wasyl often wore a homemade and handsewn sheepskin coat, which was popular attire in the village at that time.

The Samovar

Only rich people owned a samovar. It was used to make tea for visitors. The coals were placed in the center compartment, and water was poured into the belly. A container with tea was placed on top of the samovar.

On the outskirts of our village lived a rich man, who owned about two hundred acres of land. In Poland a landowner was called a *puritz*, and he was very much respected. This puritz lived in a large house with many rooms and several maids. Another building housed his workers, and a third building was a stable. Three generations lived there—the parents, the son, and the son's family. The son's two daughters didn't socialize with anybody in the village. Landowners associated only with rich people. The old man made an exception, visiting us occasionally. He liked our family.

Ukrainian Girl

The Ukrainian national costume was worn at celebrations, on holidays, and also as a wedding dress. Some girls dressed in the costume on Sunday going to church. Afterwards they would walk hand-in-hand singing songs.

The girls cross-stitched the designs on the white cotton blouses with red and black threads. My mother often made the black velvet vests. She would trace a design on the fabric and use bright-colored threads for the embroidery.

Wedding Cake

Mother baked the wedding cakes for the gentiles. This special cake consisted of white dough baked in a large baking dish twenty-five inches in diameter and about thirteen inches high. The top was decorated with roses, birds, and leaves also made of bread dough. Black herbs were used for the eyes of the birds.

The large cake was necessary, because the peasants invited everybody from the village to their weddings. The parties were held in the barn for lack of space in the house. The cake was brought in on a large tray, and the four men holding it danced in a circle and then it was served to the guests.

Surcie

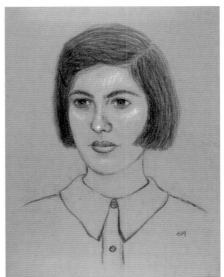

Toby

Lacjie   *Aron*

My Mother

My Father

Family Pictures

We led a primitive hard life, but we were a very close-knit family. We were not all content living in the village. It was a stigma to be a *dorfisher* (villager). Father was the only one happy on the farm. Mother would have been happier to live in the nearby shtetl, Podkamien—for the children's sake.

Surcie wanted to move to a shtetl, but her real dream was of America. I wanted to live in a shtetl to get a higher education instead of becoming a dressmaker as my father wanted. My secret dream, though, was of becoming an artist. My brother, Aron, and sister Lajcie never expressed their feelings.

But our dreams and hopes were shattered when World War II began.

The Russian Occupation

The Sounds of War

On September 1, 1939, I was awakened by a loud bugle sound. Both churches in our village rang all their bells for a long time. I asked what was happening. Mother told me the bad news in a quivering voice: it was the alarm for war. It was a sad day. We were scared and didn't know what to expect. Soon enough we heard the sounds of bombardment from Brody, a nearby city, some twenty kilometers away. Our village wasn't directly affected, and we only saw the airplane formations in the sky.

People stocked up on sugar, salt, and kerosene for the lamps. Later there was even a rumor that the Polish president, Ignacy Mościcki, passed through our village, fleeing the country.

Opening the Jail

The Nazis occupied western Poland, while the Russians took over eastern Poland. In about two weeks, our region was occupied by the Russians without incident. Communists who were jailed before the war in Poland were freed. It was frightening to hear that criminals and murderers were also released from jail if they claimed to be Communists. The poor became government officials without any knowledge of how to govern. Rich people were sent to Siberia and their houses given to the poor. Some rich people bribed the officials so they could stay in Poland. There was also a food shortage, but it didn't affect us much because we grew most of our food on the farm. Supplies such as kerosene and sugar became difficult to obtain. Under the Communists, private businesses were closed. The business owners hid their merchandise and later bartered it for food with the farmers.

Going to a Dance

When the Russian soldiers marched into our vicinity, they went on a shopping spree. They bought all the watches and clothing and lingerie they could get. The officers had their wives come to where they were stationed. These women thought that the fancy lingerie was for party dresses, and they would dress up in nightgowns and wear them to their dances.

The soldiers also bragged about the big factories they had in Russia. When asked if they had oranges in Russia, they would say, "Oh, we have big factories of oranges." They didn't even know what an orange was.

Meeting

Problems started when the Communist peasants in our village tried to encourage everyone to join the Communist Party. Families were having tremendous disagreements. There were Communist meetings held in the center of the village. Mother was in a real dilemma. Before the war, since there were no restaurants, the village mayor would pay Mother to cook the meals when he entertained government officials. Therefore, she became friendly with the local police and officials. When the Communists came, the officials felt that as a show of support, she should become involved with the new government. If Mother didn't attend the Communist meetings, she could be labeled anti-Russian, and that meant being sent to Siberia. If she did attend, she would be taken as a Communist, and she didn't want that either.

Komsomolki

In school, I had my own problems. I learned Russian, and the education was much better, but I was encouraged to join the Komsomolki, the Communist youth organization. Since I wasn't a Communist, I didn't want to join, and the two Russian teachers resented it. At a recital in the social hall, the Komsomolki, with red scarves around their necks, stood in the center of the stage, while I and two other girls were pushed to the side. I remember feeling very hurt and scared.

My Cousin Pesia

In spite of the rumors that the Jews were mistreated in Warsaw, my cousin Pesia Lewaj wanted to be reunited with her husband. She said that no matter what happened, she wanted them to be together. After the Germans occupied Warsaw, she and her three children escaped the city and with luck crossed the border into Russian-occupied Poland. They went to her mother in Brody. Her husband was supposed to follow, but he was detained. After a few months the Russian authorities asked those people who came from German-occupied Poland to register and said that they would be able to join their families. My cousin Pesia registered herself and her children. They were labeled as traitors and in the middle of the night were arrested and sent to Siberia. At that time it seemed terrible. But although they suffered greatly from cold, starvation, and hard work, my cousin and her family escaped the Nazi terror and survived.

Discussion

We got used to the way of life under the Russians. We considered ourselves lucky when, by word of mouth, we heard stories that in German-occupied Poland the Jews were ridiculed. Possessions were taken away from people, and the beards of pious old Jews were cut off by Germans in the streets. When the Germans continued invading other countries, people started talking about running away to Russia rather than sitting and waiting for Hitler to come. My father and others said that the Germans were looking for doctors and lawyers, not farmers like us. My mother and Surcie were willing to leave, but Father refused. He didn't want to leave the farm. He was set in his ways.

The German
Occupation

Yom Kippur in the Woods

In the summer of 1941 the Nazis marched into our village. They drove in on three-seated motorcycles with their neat uniforms and shiny boots. A young soldier talked to us, assuring us that they wouldn't harm anyone. However, soon enough there were several raids. First the Nazis ordered the Jews to bring out all their gold and silver. Later the Nazis came to get men for work camps. Most of the time the village officials, who were friends of my parents, tipped us off that the Nazis were coming to the village. We then warned the other Jews. Just before Yom Kippur, our friends told us that a raid was to be expected.

On Yom Kippur, we all went to the woods to hide. Mother, my sisters, and I went in one direction; Father and my brother went the opposite way. Roaming in the woods, we all met toward evening. Mother said it was meant to be that we should all be together on Yom Kippur.

In Jail

In addition to taking the men away to work camps, the Nazis ordered all the Jewish farmers to deliver most of the wheat they grew. However, if we had given them all the wheat they asked for, we would have starved. This time when my parents were warned that the Germans were coming, they went to the woods to hide. My father thought that the Germans wouldn't hurt young people, so my sisters and I were left in the barn to shred the wheat. When the Germans arrived, we explained to them that Father had delivered part of the wheat tax and couldn't deliver any more because the family had to be fed. The three of us were arrested. We spent three weeks in jail in Brody. Mother bribed some of the local officials who managed the jail, and we were released. We were told that in another week we would have been sent to a concentration camp. We had heard about the work camps but knew little of the concentration camps.

Going to the Ghetto

In the fall of 1942 the Nazis ordered my family along with the other Jews to leave our homes to go to the Brody ghetto. All the Orthodox men were forced to shave off their beards. For my father this was a big humiliation. We packed all our belongings on two wagons that the local village officials had sent us. We mostly took food, such as flour, potatoes, and beans. We gave our house to our neighbor Katerina's son. We gave our neighbors the furniture, sewing machine, and some clothing, hoping to come back after the war to claim everything. Our aunt Tema and cousin Dusia went to hide in the woods. They warned us not to go to the ghetto because they'd heard that we probably would be killed. But no one really believed that.

The Ghetto in Brody

The gentiles used to come to the barbed-wire borders of the ghetto to sell us bread and potatoes at outrageous prices. There were very few who could purchase the food, and if the German guard saw the transaction he would take away the food and beat up the poor soul.

When the Jews were thrown into the ghetto, their food was rationed meagerly. During the one-year existence of the Brody ghetto, about three quarters of the population died from starvation, disease, and cold.

Men Pulling Wagon

The two men and wagon were a daily sight on the ghetto streets. The Germans ordered the Jews to pick up their corpses. Instead of using a horse and buggy, the Germans made the Jews pull the wagon with the corpses themselves.

We, the village people, were better situated than the city people. While they were starving, we still had a supply of potatoes, wheat, and flour that we had brought from our farm.

It was very painful to watch people suffer, but we couldn't help them all. We tried to help individuals whenever we could.

Leaving My Family

In March of 1943, there was a rumor in the ghetto that the liquidation was to start the following morning. The panic was indescribable. Men and women were distraught. Some were crying, others praying. The children were confused, not fully understanding the situation. People were thinking of ways to escape. My parents didn't want to try to run away from the ghetto because Father had built a hiding place in the building we lived in that he felt would be safe. My sister Surcie was very anxious to escape and asked me to go with her. My mother encouraged me to do so. It was very difficult leaving the rest of my family for the first time in my life.

Escaping

After the painful separation, and not knowing whether we would see our loved ones again, we ran down into the dark streets wearing large gray shawls, disguised as peasants. All we had for nourishment were some pieces of sugar my mother had put in our pockets. We left in the middle of the night and were lucky there were no guards around when we crawled under the barbed wire and successfully escaped the ghetto.

Climbing Out of the Cellar

As my sister and I walked in the dark bitter-cold night through the city streets outside the ghetto, we got panicky and jumped down into the cellar of a bombed-out building. We stayed there twenty-four hours, sustaining ourselves with the sugar Mother had given us. The next evening we heard no shooting and decided to leave the city. We couldn't stay there without any food.

In order to get out of the broken-down cellar with no steps, my sister stepped on my back to reach the street. She pulled me up afterward.

Walking Through the Fields

My sister and I walked for hours through fields on a cold miserable snowy winter night and became disoriented, losing the direction of our village. We followed a small light in the distance to a farm and slept there in the barn. The next day the farmer showed us the road to Czernica.

Then our ordeal truly began. We fought for our lives, living in fear every moment of the day and night, in cold, in rain, and at times with no food at all. This terror lasted for me a whole year.

Surcie

Surcie and I became separated. When we met in the woods several weeks later, she said to me that she couldn't bear it. "I will go back to the ghetto to get Father to come to the village and build a hiding place in the woods so we can all hide together."

Arriving in the ghetto, she found everyone still alive, but Lajcie was in the hospital with typhoid fever. The conditions were terrible. The beds were filthy and without sheets. The patients had lice even in their eyebrows. So Mother and Surcie stayed to care for her. They couldn't leave.

Finally they did liquidate the ghetto, and Surcie ran away again. This time she got Mother to go with her. Surcie was so anxious to survive. Thanks to my sister, Mother and I both got out of the ghetto.

At Karolczycha's

It was May 1943 when the liquidation of the ghetto began. Mother and Surcie hid in the cellar of a ghetto building. They actually buried themselves there. With their bare hands they dug into the ground and covered the shawls on their backs with earth and lay there motionless. They heard the Germans running around the cellars calling, *Juden heraus!* ("Jews, come out!") But they were not discovered. My sister was very nervous and later decided to look for a better place to hide. We never heard from her again. The next night Mother snuck out of the ghetto cellar and came to the village. I met her at Karolczycha's house, where we hid separately. Karolczycha, the village healer, was a good friend of Mother's.

Burning Hospital

At the liquidation of the Brody ghetto all the Jews were taken to the Majdanek concentration camp. Some were lucky to escape to the woods, or they were hidden by farmers in the villages. Those caught hiding in the ghetto were shot on the spot. My father hid in the attic of the house where we lived in the ghetto. After three days without food and water he came out of hiding and was caught right away by an SS man. Sara Geller was hiding in the same attic. She heard my father ask the SS man, "Before you shoot me, can I have a drink of water?" The SS man shot my father right there. Sara Geller survived with her two children and told me about the last moments of my father's life. The people that were in the ghetto hospital had the most tragic deaths. The hospital was burned with all the people in it. The SS men shot any Jew who tried to run out of the burning building. My sister Lajcie was among those who perished.

Searching for Food

During the winter I hid anyplace that I could get into—barns, cellars, pigsties, pantries. In the summer, it was easier. I sat in the fields between tall crops and in the woods. For many days at a time I would sit on the edge of the woods in the bushes because it wasn't one of the obvious places that would be searched by the Germans or the Polish and Ukrainian police. When it rained it was horrible, but I sat through many rainy days, soaked to the bone. At night I went to the peasants, dried my clothes, got some food, and next morning went back to the woods to get soaked again! At times I wanted to give up, but the will to survive was strong.

Hiding with Friends

Once I found some friends in the woods. It was nice to be with people after hiding for months alone, but I was invaded by lice. The ground where these people spent months, day and night, was padded with leaves to protect them from the deep-wood dampness. These leaves were infested with big white lice, which I had never seen before. The lice were worse than the loneliness! I returned to the village to hide alone, where I could wash out my shirt once in a while.

Eating Hot Soup

Hot soup was a treat. I got it only once every few months when I stayed with Karolczycha. She was truly a wonderful human being. She hid first my sister and then my mother and me for a week at a time. Others would only let us stay one night, although they always gave us a chunk of bread. There were two extremes among the peasants: those who believed in helping their neighbor in need, and those who were full of hatred and would kill you because you were a Jew.

There were very, very few people who helped. Thank God for those good souls.

Aron Arrested

My brother, Aron, was taken from the ghetto to a work camp. He ran away from the camp with a friend, and they were caught by a forest watchman while hiding near our village. I too was caught by a forest watchman, but he was distracted when he saw other people running through the woods in the early dawn, and I was able to get away. Aron wasn't as lucky.

Hiding in the Attic

The last few weeks before the liberation I hid in the attic of an abandoned house. The mice kept me company, but they weren't too kind, they ate my chunk of bread at night. Therefore, I hung it on a string from the ceiling and left it there while I slept. In the straw roof was a hole and that was my window to the free world. I remember seeing the first Russian soldier walk through the village. I thought I would never see that day—Liberation Day!

Liberation

Leaving Czernica

I stood in the attic, numbed, afraid to go down in daylight. I was lucky my mother also survived by hiding in different places in the same village.

I don't remember the moment when we were reunited on Liberation Day, but I remember that when we passed our farm, leaving the village, Mother said to me, "We will probably never come back to our house again." Over the next months, in various places, we waited anxiously, hoping to hear that Father, my sisters and brother were alive somewhere. Eventually, Mother and I had to face the reality that nobody else had survived.

Walking between Bullets

Mother and I walked toward Podkamien, with the tracer bullets flying across the fields in front of us. In Podkamien we met a few Jews who had survived by hiding in bunkers in the woods. We all stayed in one house that used to belong to a Jewish family. These people got some potatoes from their neighbors and cooked soup for all of us. We tried to recover from the shock of being free.

All of a sudden we learned that the Russian army was retreating, and we were advised to follow them to avoid the return of the Germans. We felt protected by the Russian soldiers. It was the end of March 1944, and a big snowstorm developed. We struggled in the deep snow with rags tied around our feet and torn shoes. Some were lucky to get a ride in a horse and buggy. At dusk we reached Podchajew. Some people gave us food and shelter, and the next day we continued to Kremieniec, following the Russian army.

German Prisoners of War

While marching to Kremieniec, Mother and I found ourselves walking next to a group of German prisoners of war. They were surrounded by Russian soldiers who kept rifles pointed at them. We thanked God that we had lived to see those Nazi murderers as prisoners. We communicated to the Russian soldiers that we were Jews and that we had just come out of hiding. One of the soldiers asked me (probably in jest), "Here is a rifle, do you want to shoot one of the Germans?" Even if he had been serious, I knew I couldn't kill another living creature. In as much pain and anguish as we were over losing our family and relatives, and at how much the Nazis had destroyed our lives and our souls, I couldn't take another life.

Begging

In Kremieniec we met a few other survivors, some of whom had also retreated from the Hociska region. About fifteen boys and girls were staying in an empty two-room house formerly owned by Jews. Mother and I asked them if we could stay with them, and we were told, "If you can find a place on the floor to sleep, you're welcome to stay." Now we had a place to stay but no food, no work, no agency to turn to, so we all went begging for food. As we returned with our bundles, everyone compared notes to see who was a better beggar. I didn't like that and kept on asking for work. After a few days of begging, a kind woman, Mrs. Kamajewa, offered me a job taking care of her two children for room and board. Mother and I didn't want to be separated, and out of pity she took us both. Mother cleaned and cooked, and later made homemade brown soap, sold it at the market, and gave the money to Mrs. Kamajewa.

Working in the Bakery

There was a typhoid epidemic soon after the liberation, and most of the boys and girls were hospitalized and their hair shaved off. When I got sick, Mrs. Kamajewa kept me at home, and her father, a doctor, treated me free of charge.

After a few weeks the other survivors were earning some money selling home-baked rolls and yeast on the open market, but I couldn't leave Mrs. Kamajewa. She had been so kind to us when we were desperate. Sadly, her younger son got sick and died. Soon after that we left.

I got a job in an army bakery. Once I asked my supervisor, a soldier, if I could get bread to take home. His reply was, "I couldn't give it to you, but if you come wearing a large shawl, you could take home a loaf of bread and the guard wouldn't notice it." I followed his advice. The second time I took a loaf under each arm. I sold one to get some money. A little stealing was a fact of life.

Hitchhiking

From Kremieniec, Mother and I moved to Dubno to join our cousins Jakob and Ester Knobel. They had survived in the woods with a five-year-old daughter. We shared a room with them. There my mother sold salt on the open market. My friend and I imported it because salt was in great demand.

The two of us would hitchhike a ride with the Russian Army trucks (a common transportation at the time) to Lwow, a hundred kilometers away. We bought a fifteen-kilo (thirty-pound) sack of salt each, and hitchhiked back.

I tried to get in touch with our relatives in America. When we were leaving our home to go to the ghetto, I had sewed into my jacket my aunt Sarah's address in New York. In Dubno I tried to salvage that worn-out piece of paper. I wrote a letter with an incomplete address. A few months later we received a package. What a joy and moral uplift it was to be in touch with our American relatives.

I Want My Mommy

Jakob's sister Dusia had left her two-year-old son Srulek with a peasant woman in Czernica before going into hiding, and paid her to keep him. After liberation the woman sent a message to Jakob in Dubno that he should pick up the little boy because she could hardly feed her own children. This was unlike some Christians who didn't want to return the Jewish children.

Jakob picked up the little boy. He was undernourished and full of sores and lice. Jakob and Ester cleaned him, fed him, dressed him, and we gave him all the attention we could, but the child cried that he wanted his mommy! How sad it was to watch him: he didn't remember his real mother, who had been killed just a week before liberation. The only mother Srulek knew was the woman who took care of him for seventeen months! I never saw him with a smile on his face. His father survived in Russia, and they were reunited in Israel.

At the Station

Since we'd heard that some people had been killed in the villages when they returned to claim their possessions, we knew we could not go to our home. It was difficult to make an honest living in eastern Poland under the Russian occupation, so we decided to return to western Poland. With cousin Jakob we traveled to Bytom. After losing our family, relatives, and friends, we were hoping to be reunited with my mother's sister Sarah and her brothers in America.

In Bytom, we joined an illegal transport going to a DP (displaced persons) camp in West Germany. On the Czechoslovak border we were arrested and sent to Moravská Ostrava, where we were placed in crowded barracks and guarded. We slept in bunk beds, a few hundred men, women, and children, all thrown together. After a few months Joint (the American Jewish Joint Distribution Committee) intervened, and we were sent to the DP camp in Poking, West Germany.

Mother in a Wheelchair

From the DP camp at Poking, a rural region in West Germany, Mother and I transferred to the DP camp at Föhrenwald near Munich. There at the HIAS (Hebrew Immigrant Aid Society) office I registered to emigrate to America. We were told again and again of the long wait.

In the meantime my mother suffered a stroke. I was told she had only a few months to live. My hopes were shattered again.

Later my mother was transferred to a hospital for the chronically ill in Bad Wörishofen. After two years she was recovering slowly. With her sister and brothers' guarantee to support her in the United States, Mother was able to emigrate and was reunited with her family in New York after thirty-seven years. The doctor who treated my mother in Germany said it was a miracle that she was alive. She lived for sixteen more years.

The Kitchen and Social Hall at Föhrenwald

The DP camp Föhrenwald was governed by the survivors, as were all the DP camps. We were supported by UNRRA (United Nations Relief and Rehabilitation Administration) and by Joint. Two and three families shared a room, separated from one another by army blankets. At the beginning, food was cooked at a central kitchen. Later we received rations of dry food and canned goods. We had two electric burners in the room. A management office gave out clothes and blankets, and assigned rooms and the very few jobs that were available.

We had our own police, a hospital, a doctor and two nurses, a Hebrew and Yiddish school for the children, and an ORT (Organization for Rehabilitation), a trade school for adults. Dressmaking, tailoring, and electronics courses were attended by many to prepare themselves for better jobs in their prospective countries. Many people were active in various Zionist organizations.

The Clown

In the social hall we had movies, a concert sometimes, or the Hebrew school students put on a play. There were dances organized for the youth. We also used to attend lectures given by the Zionist organizations. But it was a real lift to our morale when the American actors of the Jewish stage came to entertain us. I remember Herman Yablkow's performance in *Der Piac* ("The Clown"). I had never before seen a Jewish show and was very impressed with the performance.

Starting a New Life

L ife in the DP camp was frustrating. It was very discouraging to wait from one year to the next to get out of bloodstained Europe. There was a joke in the camp, *Gdzie jedziesz ja pojade* ("Where are you going? Emigrating? I'm coming along"). People registered for whatever country they could emigrate to—the United States, Argentina, Australia. There were also illegal transports to Israel. Some people from Föhrenwald left with the *Exodus* and landed in Cyprus.

In spite of all the problems, many people were getting married, having babies, trying to rebuild their lives.

My Engagement

In 1949 I lived in Bad Wörishofen, where my mother was in the DP hospital. We were next in line for immigration to America.

Many girls who had already gotten to America wrote to their friends in the DP camp that it was very hard to meet boys in the giant city of New York. The word got around, and many boys and girls in the DP camps got married, some out of convenience.

I met my future husband at the hospital seder, which he conducted. He noticed me when I, being the youngest there, opened the door for Elijah. We immediately liked each other and kept company. Four months later we got engaged and decided to take out a marriage license from the town hall, enabling my future husband to get a visa for America. The religious ceremony was to take place when we arrived in New York.

The Wedding

W e had lived through so much tragedy, my mother looked forward to the joy of her only surviving daughter's wedding. Mother was now living with her brothers in New York. She sensed their concern about the expense of making a wedding for us when we arrived there, so in a letter Mother advised us to get married in the DP camp in order not to be a burden to the family.

My friend Genia Prawer and her sister Pola made the wedding for us in their house in Landsberg. They borrowed the white skirt and white blouse that many girls in the DP camp got married in.

My Family

After four years in the DP camp, my husband and I finally reached the United States in December 1949. We were reunited with my mother and other American relatives in the Bronx. A year later my daughter, Lillian, was born.

Most people emigrated to the new state of Israel, a lifelong dream becoming a reality. In spite of Hitler's plans to annihilate all the Jews, the small remnant of us who survived started new lives in new countries, building new families, hoping for a better future for our children and their children.

Acknowledgments

From Toby Knobel Fluek, for the original edition

It is not possible to mention everyone who helped me with this book, but I do want to thank some people especially:

My husband, Max, for his love and patient understanding.

My daughter, Lillian, and her husband, Steve, for their encouragement, support, and help with the writing.

My editor, Ann Close, for her enthusiasm, kindness, and belief in my book, and of course my agent, Julian Bach, who had confidence in my story and felt it should be published.

Steve Schoenholtz, Morton Yarmon, and Lucjan Dobroszycki, who guided me with the manuscript; Judy Schloss Markowitz, who helped me with the editing; and Eve Diana, for the many hours she spent working on it at the word processor.

My art teacher, Joe Hing Lowe, who shared his knowledge so unselfishly; Irene Roth, whose assistance and criticism of my paintings were invaluable; and Ruth Schloss, who frequently posed for me while I worked.

Tony Holmes, who photographed the paintings for this volume; Mia Vander Els, who designed the book; and Andy Hughes, who oversaw its production.

Genia Kutner, Joe Prawer, Florence Chasin, Lillian Kurz, Rachel Kaufman, Dorothy Miller, and Sadie Kwait for helping me in various ways. And Lottie Geller Wiesel, Jack Wiesel, Asher and Eva Richter, Clara Posner and her late husband, Chaim Posner, and Simon and Sheila Zwany, who helped by reaffirming my memories about life in the old country.

From Lillian Fluek Finkler, Toby Knobel Fluek's daughter, for this edition

I would like to thank my dear friend Dr. Rakhmiel Peltz for writing the foreword to this new edition of my mother's book. Dr. Peltz encouraged my mother and recognized the value and the importance of her story and artwork in teaching about the Jewish way of life in Poland before the Holocaust. His documentary film, *Toby's Sunshine*, and website, Alive! (alivetobyssunshine.com), bring her legacy to life.

Thank you to Erin Blankenship and her colleagues at The Florida Holocaust Museum (FHM; thefhm.org) for curating, preserving, and exhibiting my mother's artwork, which is now part of the FHM's permanent collection. Through the exhibits at the museum and via its website, her art is available to the public and schools for the current and future generations.

And thank you to Matthew Lore and his colleagues, including Beth Bugler, Pamela Schechter, Zach Pace, Hannah Matuszak, and Anthony Cardellini at The Experiment for doing such an outstanding job republishing my mom's book. You have preserved and reproduced her work beautifully while at the same time enhancing the book's design. What a gift to the world!

About the Author

TOBY KNOBEL FLUEK (1926–2011) was born in the eastern Polish village of Czernica. In 1942, she and her family were forced by the Nazis into the nearby Brody ghetto. After her escape and years in hiding, she was married in 1949 and emigrated with her husband to New York, where she remained until her death.

Fluek is the subject of the documentary film *Toby's Sunshine: The Life and Art of Holocaust Survivor Toby Knobel Fluek* and is featured in *Image Before My Eyes: A History of Jewish Life in Poland Before the Holocaust*. She is also the author of *Passover As I Remember It*. Her art has been exhibited in venues including the Queensboro Community College, the Holocaust Museum & Center for Tolerance and Education at Rockland Community College, and the Bronx Museum's community gallery.

To ensure that Fluek's work would be available to current and future generations, in 2018, her daughter, Lillian Fluek Finkler, donated more than five hundred of her mother's artworks and personal items, including the majority of the art that appears in this book, to The Florida Holocaust Museum, which shares Fluek's work in exhibitions and outreach programs. Lillian and her husband, Steven; their sons, Gary and David; and their daughters-in-law and four grandchildren continue striving to ensure Toby Knobel Fluek's extraordinary legacy.

Max Fluek, David Finkler, Gary Finkler, Toby Knobel Fluek, 2006